ARABY

Araby

Eric Ormsby

SIGNAL EDITIONS IS AN IMPRINT OF VÉHICULE PRESS

For its publishing program, Véhicule Press acknowledges the on-going financial support of the Canada Council for the Arts and the Government of Canada's Book Industry Development Program.

Signal Editions editor: Carmine Starnino
Cover design: David Drummond
Photo of author: Terence Byrnes
Set in Minion by Simon Garamond
Printing: AGMV-Marquis Inc.

CANADIAN CATALOGUING IN PUBLICATION DATA

Ormsby, Eric L. (Eric Linn), 1941-
  Araby
Poems.
ISBN 1-55065-145-5

I. Title.

PS8579.R58A82 2001   c811'.54   C2001-900274-2
PR9199.3O75A82 2001

Véhicule Press
www.vehiculepress.com

Distributed in Canada by General Distribution Services.
Distributed in the United States by LPC Group.

Printed in Canada on alkaline paper.

For David Solway

ومن لم يعشق الدنيا قديماً ولكن لا سبيل الى الوصال

"Who has not loved the world from of old?
And yet, there is no way to be one with it."

– Abu Tayyib al-Mutanabbi

Contents

"To make the ear
of the *khinzîr*
(that grotty pig!)
lustrous
as the Pleiades…"

Jaham pondered this and said:
Rather, to make the ears
of the Pleiades
pig-like, that is, porous, gristle-
webbed, conical, tendril-

attuned to the earth.

THE FATHER OF CLOUDS

Jaham in the Autumn Rains

The Father of Clouds sat surrounded by coffee beans
and the odor of roasting coffee filled the room.
When the beans had been ground and steeped
he poured the coffee the color of fresh blood
into the *baharjiyah* and the spice-pot fumed.
Scent of cardamom wheedled the hard-edged air.

In November, he said, God's angel herds the clouds
and drives them forward with a whistling stick.
Then, he said, the Sisters rule the night
and the fattening rains begin.

In autumn, when the signs of rain appear,
I can compose my verse. I drive the syllables
before me, I call *hâb hâb* to the clouds
of my words, I gather them in tumultuous
corrals. The colts of my sinuous vowels
tug against the leather of my consonants.

At sunset, in November, when the Pleiades
appear, after the arid rule of Canopus,
my rough herd moves in concert
to the stars of rain.

Bald Adham

Bald Adham, Jaham's sidekick, was a sleek
grease-monkey from Jizan, that hell
hole on the Red Sea where the cats
tiptoe with tails atilt down pitted streets.

In Jizan, cockeyed town, everything tilts:
the whitewashed minarets decline like dials
on sunstruck clocks, the windows lean
their woozy panes at angles to the lanes,
the alleyways are twisted with declivities,
and in the oil-smudged surf flamingos tilt
with stubby wings uplifted as in rough
supplication to some asymmetric god.

Bald Adham in his bandoliers of grease
hectored Jaham to join the Holy War.
Adham saw the infidel in every wing
nut and sprocket, sniffed the heretic
in air filters rounded by idolatry,
in barbaric typefaces on air-couriered crates,
blind steel impressed with bestial anagrams
in the Beelzebubic lingo of the Yanks.
Tony the Tiger spelled the End of Days
when Dajjâl would rise up with all his hordes
to lick believers' blood out of their own skull-cups.
The infidel is everywhere, he growled. He spat
dreadful imprecations as he overhauled
staggered transmissions and sprained modulator valves.

Jaham humored his friend. Theology, he thought,
was a tumor of reason caused by the *Jinn*.
He loathed transcendence as he loathed the clap.
He wiped the sludgy sweat from Adham's brow

until his old pal's baldness glimmered like a dome
at dawn resplendent with sweet truth, a minaret
emerging from the dubious clouds of night.
He knew his friend's horizon was askew
for in the town that spawned him, by the sea,
even the smutty shorebirds must correct the sky.

Bald Adham Says his Prayers

At midnight, Adham crawled out of bed
and held a loud palaver with the Lord
of both the worlds. He unrolled his prayer rug,
thinned to tatters where his forehead
rubbed against the fabric as he bowed
and pitted where his supplicating knees
fulcrumed his prostrations. Adham kowtowed
melodically, both palms beside both ears,
with yips of praise and howls of accolade,
his brow abased and his hindquarters high,
and sang out words the centuries
that intervened between the Messenger and us
had scoured to such a shine
they glimmered with anonymity.
Adham never asked his Lord for anything.
His tongue coiled about each spittle-
burnished syllable with a quickened
lick of love, his prayer a cat
that purrs with praises as it brisks its pelt.

There was a pleasure for him in the nights
he lavished on invisible
blandishments and shadow lauds.
His prayer became a house
in which each window was an ardent vowel
lighting the casement that it then consumed.

And when he felt the night grow burdensome
Adham bawled a final cantillation
whose hot vehemence made the roof beams creak.
Muezzin of impetuous minarets,
he sobbed cadenzas that assailed the heights
to seduce God into daybreak once again.

Jaham Divines

Jaham listened to auguries and yarrow stalks.
He read the will of God from the groins of dunes.
The armpits of arroyos told him where
the lovingkindness of Allah had hid
groundwater for his camel calf to lap
out of the branded goblet of his palm.
He reverenced the knees of creosote
bushes and the shoulder blades acacias
promenade beneath the lustful moon.
He read the future from encrypted
messages the bones on badlands left.
He trusted in the alphabets of stars,
the syllabaries of the fretful clouds.

At night, when the hungry moon began
to howl, Jaham listened. He could swear
he heard the scritch of a black ant
upon the pumice of an ancient lake,
could hear the breathing of the ant,
could time its cadences, could calibrate
the secret collocation of its mandibles
as he prayed in darkness for the grain of light
it carried in its pincers to its lair.
Jaham felt his own heart start to beat
in subterranean clicketings of hope:
he tasted the rain in granaries of cloud
and learned the silos where the winds are stored.

An Old Poet Bites

When he was fourteen Jaham got
the mystic mantle of his poetry.
The luminescent prosody
of a dying master
came down to him one day.

Jaham paid a visit to the bard.
The bard was portly and avuncular,
nibbled on pears and pomegranates as
they chatted, but was failing fast.

When Jaham went to leave, the poet
crooked a plump index finger at him, croziered
him over to the bedside where he urged
Jaham to bend close, bend closer, near his mouth.

With unexpected vigor the old man
sank two sharp incisors into the boy
– into his sweet and nearly speechless mouth –
and chawed him like an elapid,
working the poison well into his skin,
gnawing at his mouth till the hot bite
brought blood. And then he said:

The only antidote is in the bite.

Jaham went home writhingly and learned to write.

Jaham on the Conquests of Childhood

North of a bottle cap lay Samarqand.
With pocketknives we divvied up the spoils.

With lances made of windshield wipers or of broken brooms
We hunted mighty Yazdegird to earth,
We cut his kingly throat, we stuck his head
On a creaking gatepost where his satraps stood.

East of a punctured inner tube there burned
The brazen furor of Heraclius.

West of the blear-eyed aggies in their pungent bag
We brought the terrible Berbers underfoot
And sailed on matchbox triremes through the Straits.

South of a slingshot made of forking twigs
And held together by a twanging band,
We saw the archipelagoes of the newborn day
And unimaginable peoples coursing there.

Beyond the tire pit Ecbatana shone.

Jaham and his Cat

The pink melodious ratchet of her tongue
psalmodized as she hunched on Jaham's chest.
Jaham admired her reverence of repose,
the prayerful alertness of her ears,
the pierced opacity of her green eyes
whose irises held aloof the more they shone,
her silken dignity, the way she made
a pedestal of paw to rest upon
behind a twitching balustrade of tail.

To drink he gave her pungent camel's milk
he bought at the Desert's Edge Convenience Store.
Jaham listened, he heard her chant Qur'an
in purr-cadenzas of complicit calm.
The cat sang *Allah   Allah   Allah*
and made her chant sound natural as breath.

Was she some subtle prophetess of sleep,
a disciple of our Prophet (may God
pray for him!), who once had said:
People are sleeping;
when they die, they wake?

He remembered how Muhammad cut his cloak
rather than dislodge a dozing cat.
All night he let her murmur on his breast,
all night her coiled contentment lulled his rest.

Jaham Serenades a Snake

O patterned psychopomp,
all spiral tail and curlicue of gait,
all accent-lashed, all circumspect of hip,
teach me hollow inside hollow
where the magnet mind can't follow!
Your hunch and crumple progress down a slope
has the topple look of hope,
the spillgate promise of the brimming cup,
even as you coil your selves down our thorny dunes,
fumy as ectoplasm with an ambient
emollience of sand.
                          I saw its whipping autograph
surmount the idle and mellifluous stub
of the tail. I saw the swallower swallowed in the loam
hollow of itself as fingertip in fawn
glove is gowned and fragrantly transformed.
I saw its virgule sassiness embrangle earth.
I thought:
Poor sheepskin! Poor certificate! But the nimble
bureaucrat inverts itself while we
salute a serpent tail tip from the Cherokee.

I know
your snake's tongue semaphores some question
to us. Your sleek lip interrogates our air.
You know the hidden bodies of our family
for you have sucked their bones for prey.
You twined the eye sockets of my grand-dad's
skull, you slid and you insinuated in
the pelvis of my mother and my aunt, you
circumambulated all the buried bones
the way a bearded pilgrim throngs about

the midnight meteorite in the silver clasp
of the Kaʿba, and if I cry aloud
only the jointed rosary of your vertebrae
is left for me to pray, forgetful
supplicant adoze in the warmth of the sun
from whose imperishable fingernails
the names of God will run
like blacksnakes over stones.

Jaham and the Baboons of Hada

The baboons of Hada love the heights.
High places let them contemplate
the sordid valleys they have left behind.
Along the scalded stones blue lizards lie,
flatten themselves or pump their beaded throats,
but the baboons of Hada are aloof:
The baboons know the indifference of peaks;
even their antics are deliberate;
their skipping over crags has stateliness.

I like the way the baboons of the heights
have colonized the coldest pinnacle,
have softened and made stoical and sly
the summits where five stringy crows still wheel,
have humorized abysses, made crevasses
comical, vaudevilleaned the avalanche.
Now the sweet sisters groom their brothers' braids,
old aunties coif the mustaches of nieces;
their bright fastidious molars crackle mites.

And all the while one Abrahamic ape,
the dominant, the doge of his troupe,
hunkers heraldic on a lip of stone.
His silvery Hamitic sideburns fluff
in the breezes of the heights. He shuts both eyes.
The patriarch of Hada shuts his eyes
and all around is sibilance and gust.
The scavenger baboons, consanguinous,
plump down on their buttocks in the calm.

A sense of fullness rises with the dusk.
Five crows still quarrel at contested scraps
but the lord of foragers is throned in peace

amid the frisky chittering of his kids.
The baboons wait until the rocks of heights
become supernal in the full moon's light.
At nightfall the baboons of Hada sit
in chuckling circles where they contemplate
the radiant bottom of the risen moon.

(al-Ta'if, July 1997)

The Egyptian Vulture

"Egyptian Vultures are well known as being
the least discriminating of scavengers."
– W. E. Cook, *Avian Desert Predators*

The Egyptian Vulture is the least
discriminating of the scavengers.
He sucks up eyeball juice of wildebeest
as though it were iced Bollinger.

He spreads a gray paté of rotted gnu
on a barfed-up bed of jungle turkey comb.
Raw rectum of gazelle is *cordon bleu*
yet how piously he dines, with plumed aplomb!

The stomach contents of some ripe giraffe
pleasure him more than freshly slivered truffles.
He stuffs his whole head in and you hear him laugh
as he snacks on gassy guts and belly ruffles.

Would you really call him *indiscriminate*?
True, his topknot is fouled with shit and bile
(unavoidable when you work your snout in straight
up the flyblown butt of some long-dead crocodile)

but see how he grooms himself when his chow is done:
He hangs his litigious pinions out to air,
he preens his turban till it's debonair,
he strops his beak in the Egyptian sun.

At the Ruins of Recollection

Bald Adham and Black Mary

Despite his orthodoxy Adham fell
for a cockeyed girl among the infidel.

Black Mary with her Abyssinian
mincing and her deftly fluttered dulcimer
she strummed all evening with a supple whir
tortured him at his prayers. Callipygean
promise wafted from her rosepetal-seamed ʿabâya
and yet, she was uncleaner than a hound,
thick with fleas of heresy and ticks of doubt.

One night she offered him fresh-sliced papaya
on a silver tray. Her tattooed toes peeped out
under her hem. Adham sighed. He pawed the ground.
He snorted like a stallion led to stud.
Black Mary drew him down into the sweet pink mud
behind the body shop and wrapped him in her veils.
In the name of God! He roared and lipped her breasts.
Praise to the Creator! Adham thundered as her nails
dug into the bare flesh of his back and sinuous gusts
of some Djibouti perfume cloaked his throat, his nose.
Glory Glory be to God! Bald Adham stammered
as he mounted Black Mary and then entered her,
a drugged bee asprawl in a nectarous rose.

Let me instruct you in the Path of Truth! he yammered
but Black Mary wound him in a silken blur,
enlaced and wove and filamented him in silicate
strands more delicate
than the gossamer
flounces orioles confect on summer boughs.

Adham could not extricate
his limbs from hers, his breath from the drowse
of her breath on his throat, and so they lay,
orthodox and infidel, until the white thread of day,
that moiré glimmer on the satin-stitch of night,
could just be distinguished by its own merged light.

Adham Sings of Internal Combustion

The crankshaft sucks the piston to its brink
and then the camshaft opens up the valves.
I love to let the anointed piston sink
down towards the flywheel in the engine block.

The air-brimmed fuel is drawn into the cylinder
and at the last plunge of the piston's strike
the intake valves fall closed and so surrender.
The crankshaft slides the piston through the cylinder
and enters in and occupies and salves
the block with dizzy vapors from the chamber
where lightning-frictioned sweet combustion tinders
the spark plugs' effervescence of ignition.

I love the vaporous and thrummed cognition
the engine block surrenders as it comes
to full exhaustion in the flywheel's spoke.

I love the crankshaft's spin just when emission
kindling the engine's cycle re-engenders
propulsion while the crankshaft hones its screws.

O there's a cadence to the slicked machine!
There is a sweet-greased music to the cylinder!

I love the snug piston whose dense gasoline
ambrosial with oxygen now renders,
in frothy plunges, as the flywheel spins,

strummed spasms of combustion to the engine block.

Love among the Dunes

When Jaham fell in love his skin became
xylophonic. Each fingertip would ping,
each dimple vocalize till all his body chimed.
His toenails clicked their little castanets,
his ankles and patella cadence-clacked,
his piccolo of penis piped its glee,
his nipples pizzicattoed with a taut
epidermal anthem of delight,
and even his shy balls in their goathair sack
blipped like muffled bugles when he walked.

His tongue alone was thronged with silences.
His mouth was deader than a soldered flute,
his teeth chatterless as a sprained harmonium.
Even his garrulous eyeballs had turned dumb.

But when love came to him, that leopard-whelp
with dark lope and both wild eyes
like pristine puddles where blue cyclones loom,
his very gooseflesh crooned to the dunes

in phosphor aureoles of synaptic song.

Jaham Deciphers the Scripts of Insomnia

O stars that calligraph my sleeplessness!
All night your delicate nibs have filigreed
the virgin blackness of the southern sky
with sly epistles in a chancery hand
and I lie open-eyed, heart athud, my mind
straining to decipher your shrewd strokes.
I see a sudden swoop-shaped vowel
gild the parchment of a scrolling cloud,
or then heat-lightning puffs the page
with flocks of full-stops and I stammer there,
my palate thistled by the scripted sky.

Night is a block of solid black,
night is a cube, a *ka'ba*, a chunk
of another world behind our world.
Night is a holy dense irreducible
pebble draped in a sumptuous covering,
needlepointed with the consonants of God,
birdwinged with startled vowels.

And under the Ptolemaic helices of heaven
the moon is a pudgy scribe who dabs
unctuous letters on the pumice clouds.
A lazy, lolling, word-infested scribe
whose fingers, disciplined in indolence,
stipple bright *fathas*, opulent *dammas*,
kasras piercing as the fang of dawn,
along the vellum of the midnight sky.
Sleeplessly I follow the plump moon's reed
pen as it dwindles and then upswells.
I hate the fat moon with a fierce affection,

I hate how he doodles on the anthracite
immaculate darkness with his stub of a pen,
one studious drop of radiance
quilling its fertile tip.

Mrs. Jaham

> "In my youth I married a ghoul
> Who resembled a gazelle."
>
>   – al-Jahiz, *The Book of Animals*

One morning Bald Adham glimpsed
the naked foot of Jaham's wife as she
slipped him a cup of coffee through the flap
of the connubial tent. Despite the numerous
bangles that gave voices to her wrist,
Adham saw her foot was slipperless
and thick with a downy pelt of blackest fur.

And Adham understood then that his pal
had married not a gazelle but a ghoul,
and that his power as a poet came
from the uncanny
cloaked in a kitchen robe.

Bald Adham Falls into Heresy

Bald Adham said one day:
God is an amputee,
a disincarnate Hand
aslant the sky It papered and drew taut.
He wouldn't recant but later claimed:
God is a sandstorm made of body parts,
a casual, agglomerated Thing.
Yes, God is a Thing, he said,
an object all direction but dimensionless.

Still, *God must have a bottom,* said he, *for*
He sits upon a throne ...

The next day he said: *God is a foot.*
Jaham asked him: "Does God have ten toes just like us?"
Adham answered him: *The Almighty has*
only ten toes, like us, but they are in

infinitudes of foot.

Adham Overhauls an Old Caprice

Bald Adham used a threaded damper puller
to coax the hub from the end of the crankshaft.
He took out the pulley retaining bolts
and then withdrew the breather pipes from the rocker covers.
He pondered the hairpin clip
at the bell crank, then carefully
removed that too. He swabbed the mating
surfaces of the cylinder head and rubbed them clean
with loving swipes of rag and a growled out prayer.

"My little *hubârâ*, my sweet sand grouse,"
he crooned, "You have grown old, like me."
He diagnosed his body as he diagnosed
the engine of an old Caprice. He knew
his timing chains were clanking on overtime,
his dowel-pin-chamfer was a catastrophe,
and even his camshaft sprocket, once his pride,
wobbled when he floored the pedal now.
He remembered with a blush beneath his grease
days when his steering knackle and his
stabilizer bar required
no pry tool for their maintenance.

Now, left to overhaul this elderly V-8,
he plunged his surgical fingers, gloved in sludge,
into the torque-stunned heart of the engine block.
"My dove," he sang, "My antelope,"
as he dotingly installed
new valve-cover grommets that the Infidel
had docked at Jeddah just two weeks before.
"Beloved," he hummed, "when your lugnuts gleam again
we'll tame the turnpikes and outrun our rust."

The engine shivered. Adham felt
the whomping heart fire at his fingertips.
He sensed how purringly his own
combustion chamber filled again
with the gleam of fuel.
Bald Adham kissed his grease gun and oil filter wrench
and he praised the Lord Who pricks the dead to life.

Hubble-Bubble

On Fridays Jaham smoked his hubble-bubble.
He stuffed the bowl with *hashish* smuggled in
beneath the floorboards of a Lebanese
watermelon trucker named Fu'ad.
He held a smolder to the fragrant lump.
Opulent bubbles wallowed as he drew
columns of smoke into his cloudy mouth.
Jaham dreamed of houris as he puffed,
of breasts like goblets where his thirst might sip
honeydew from rosy nipples, dreamed of thighs
ambrosial with the juices of desire
where he might stallion all paradise
and ride his wives, Jaham a lightning-bolt
piercing the fleecy negligees of clouds.

In pungent billows of aerated smoke
the hubble-bubble fed his reveries.
The more he smoked the more he felt himself
no dreamer but the insubstantial smoke
the pipe tossed with a chuckle to the air.
The hubble-bubble was umbilical
and swaddled him in cauls
of intimate myrrh. On
spanked-up cushions of upholstered smoke
Jaham inhaled the familiar, the much-loved
alleyways of towns he'd never seen.
There the souk of paradise had opened:
transfigured merchants were unspooling hanks
of spangled fabrics woven by the hands
of invisible children laughing silkily.

The Jinn

have an oily railyard lantern flame
of equivocal blaze. Sometimes, when so
inclined, the coastal jinn give off a musky
animal glow such as cat fur produces on a rainy day.
They are fond of tall tales and they cluster round
the burner when the *bunn* is being roasted
and as the magic whiff
of freshly toasted coffee beans climbs up
the hairy wall of the tent, and as tranquillity
gleams in the smug crimson of the coal,
the jinn begin to gloss the words of men.

Their speech is an incised shape of silence, an intaglio,
in which the word is not a single, schisted bloc
of sense, like ours, but guards its pristine
opacity and is impossible
for any dragoman to approximate.

We can only
struggle to imagine their colloquies,
all consonant and *sukûn*, a
gravity of gesture tinged by the fire they are,
ingot-malleable, nugget-plush, pyritic and aureate,
and yet, for all their clang,

perorating and impulsive as a flame.

Jaham Sings of the Fear of the Moon

The moon is thin with fear,
the delicate moon is thinner than despair.

The fear of the moon is the fear of the hare
curved in its burrow when the fox is near.

The fear of the moon is the fear of the fog
(The fog is afraid of the fox and the dog

and the moon is afraid of all three.)
The moon is a thorn in midnight's tree.

The moon is thin as the edge of a cry,
as fine as the side of a word.

The thin moon hides in the dark of my eye.
Night-hidden I heard

its thinness crackle like the stalks of fall
before the hail comes and the first stars fall.

Night-hidden I heard its thin feet run
away from the golden horror of the sun.

Jaham at the Ruins of Recollection

"Traces that speak not..."
                    – Zuhayr

I grieve for Mulaybid
now a scramble of ruins.
In ochre doorways the spider
has set up her loom.
In fragrant chambers
where giggling virgins henna'd their fingers
the scorpion nests her spawn.
In curtained bedrooms where the bridegroom once
laid bare the eager nipples of his bride
the jackal whelps her pups.
And from the tilting chimneys
the scribal owl recites the lineage
of children with their slate-
scratched signatures who all
have vanished from the benches of the school.

I grieve for the evenings of Turayf
whose voices wove
a fabric that the crackle
coals of the tamarisk
threaded with its aromatic
banter to a vivid silk
that mantled us. Families
squatted there with crimson
shadows of companionship
softening faces that the wind
had carved, with palms
the sands had seamed
made affable to the clasp of coffee cups.

I grieve for the voices lost
in the sift of recollection,
beyond Mulaybid where the harsh
ever-seething ridges of the Dahna rise,
past Wadi Hanifah where the wild
goats browse, past the smudge of storm-
strewn campsites whose inscriptions now my eyes
cannot decipher on the fire-scrawled cooking stones.
I grieve for the moons we once together watched,
I grieve for the moon
the unremembering sun has bled to death.

Jaham's Dream Camel

– after the Caliph Ibn al-Mu'tazz (murdered 908)

When the dawn is splashed with white like an old man's skull
I set out on my camel, full-blooded and freshly branded.
His ears resemble fronds on the naked palm
or the myrtle that towers high above the reeds.
His hoof is a downturned bowl,
black-rimmed as the inscription on a faience cup.

My stallion surpasses the aim of the widest eye.
He is quicker than water to run down polished hills.
He is quicker than heart-piercing thought
or the twisting eye-flickers of a man in doubt.

My Sherari camel is hellfire itself and he
blazes unceasingly, a tamarisk
of flame stoked by the winds of the Great Nafûd.

He is a falcon trained to the rule
that pours out on the thick-gloved hand of the falconer
a harsh and plummeting lash of punishment.

My camel is swifter than the skeptic's look.
He plunges the way rain plunges into a well.
He is skittery like the glowering augur's eye
that glimpses phantoms in damp-clodded soil.

He flies like a man who is terrified
of his own desire
and yet who chases the torture of his desire.

He never flies except toward spilling blood.

He pierces the north.

He pierces the south.

Jaham Travels West to Khemisset Oasis

The lathing of erosion on the hills
has whittled away all angularities and left
these womanly declivities and swells:
An eloquence of shoulders in the slopes
of the olive groves, velvety
insinuations that spool down
from clavicles of cherished terraces.
The leaves the olives proffer to the light
have a gravity of silver in their flourishes.
The trees receive the footprints of the breeze
that hotly steps across their canopies
like children when their mother wipes their faces
– mild but definitive.
                              The hills are sofa-brown
and plush with vinyl accents where one field's
been stitched to a neighbor's. And there are cryptic
cicatrices which a plow
impressed into the old recycled soil and these
faint scars pale at sunset with a ritual
patterning: henna-tinted, dim tattoos.
Beyond the bosomy embedded sides
of the hills the sternness of sierras
alerts the light. Dusk twinkles lethally
from riptooth peaks which guard the sea beyond
like shattered bottle-bits on garden walls.

LAST THINGS

Ramadan

A jackass was braying in the date palm grove.
By the starry watering hole
goats were browsing on the fronds
of the young palms. The billygoat,
his mufti's beard curved like the letter *lâm*,
clattered upon the mud brick parapet
and studied Jaham with his oblong eyes.
The mud-baked palaces of the emirs,
the picked bones in the cinders,
the freshly sooted surfaces of the stones,
moved Jaham more than chives in early spring
when the badlands glimmer with their bright sharp shoots.

Ramadan fell in the summer of that year.
By day they didn't eat or drink or smoke.
They didn't unhook the tent flaps of their wives.
All day they sat in the shade of the roof
or dozed on cushions with their hands
propping their chins. Remembrance came
(through expiations that the sand itself
learned in the ages before God made man)
and instructed them to parch
pious routine out of their usual bones.

When Jaham heard the call to prayer he rose
and muttered, *Lethal poison!* But when
the jackass brayed and the pariah dogs
all fell to howling he exclaimed,
These are my true muezzins!
And he prayed to God until his temples rang.

Jaham Praises

"…in prayer it is recommended that one say, 'O
Lord of heavens and earth! and not, 'O Lord of
dogs and swine,' even though He is their Lord."
    – Ibn Manzur, *Lisan al-'arab*, VI:67.

Lord, you are holy in
bloody napkins and the mouths of flies.

I praise You, Lord, not only in the disprized
pig but in the shit that cakes its trotters and its rump.

I praise You, Lord, at execution grounds
and in the neighborhood of tanneries. I
praise You in the tripes and in the bowels.

I praise you in the mandibles of bedbugs
that nip my ass and make me rise at night.
And when I rise, I make my orisons
to You, Ineffable, who gleam in turds
and tumors, in bunions and in lesions and in scabs.

Others bore the peacocks with their glozening
encomia. They wear away the roses and the beds
where narcissi bow and sway. I praise the muck
where sowbugs drowse. I praise the scurf and mold.
I praise the entities You fashioned out of
more than love – say, rather, from Your
pleasure in the obdurate and in tough
nuggets of refusal and in those inexpugnable

nuclei too uncomely for all utterance.

Jaham on the Difficult Beauty of the First White Hair

What is lovelier than the dark
when it draws the heavy curtains of the day
and beds the sun in cushions of black cloud?
A passion of blackness coronates the heads
of the young and blackness gives their skulls
that onyx glossiness. Today I found
my first white hair. How could my light
be dying when my heart
is twined by black strands to the farthest star?

As always in distress I took my refuge in
the verses of the classics where I read
what Sharif al-Radi wrote of his first white hair:

Time rubs the swordblade free of tarnishes
youth's impetuous loveliness imposes.

Caliph of Confusion

There is a tiny speck in Jaham's eye
where the Caliph of Confusion rents a room.
The Caliph is insane and loves costume.
One day a nuncio, the next an Albanian spy.
He is no principle. He is an imp.
He enacts the spasm in the woof of time
but stands for nothing at all beyond a crimp
in comprehension, that small, sublime
stammer we enunciate when sense breaks down
and the smug palate and the thuggish tongue
baffle their delphic and lubricious truths
to stuttered stillness.
                        When he was young
Jaham's eye was a perfectly pure, nut-brown
orb without a single speck and his strong
throat sang with all the certified youths
of his tribe. The Caliph was his Iblîs
– a nip of darkness in the skin of the light,
the sly flea that itches the lobes of peace –
and he taught him how to navigate the night.

A Duet with the Wolf

> "Many's the sable-gray honey-gatherer, no friend of mine,
> I've called to my fire at midnight, and he came to me…"
> — Al-Farazdaq

In the crackle light of his coals Jaham
caught the fire-shine of back-teeth.
He smelled wolf's breath.

"My wolf," he announced, "I'm holding a 30.06!"
To his surprise the wolf sang back with a rhyme:
O please let me snuggle up to your fire of sticks!

Jaham pondered and then improvised
and each of his impromptus the wary wolf revised:
"My wolf, I am old but my eye, though bleared, sees far.
With a single shot I can drill a tossed dinar."

The wolf commenced a counter-strum like a seven-stringed guitar:
My pelt's a shred, my ribs poke out, my pads are blisters.
Early senility has stippled my whiskers.
Jaham's rejoinder sidled like a twister:
"My molars shone like mosque lamps brimmed with blessed oil
and now they jut like blackened chassis from a junkyard soil.
Once they were high beams backed with lambent foil
and now glom darkly like some burnt-out fumarole…"

The wolf began a half-suppressed, resentful boil:
Your teeth! My arrogant fangs are worn down as the curbs
where knackered camels piss, they are lonely as suburbs
in bankrupt desert developments, they're feeble as the blurbs
festooning failed potboilers with inflated verbs…!

Jaham (whom no braggadocio perturbs)
feinted fiercely then and pointed to his brows:
"My eyebrows once were prickly as iron rasps
whose stiff aplomb no brusque khamsin can dowse,
my temples were the robust hasps
of teak-panelled glove compartments, my…"
                                        The wolf untous-
led his tongue and contralto'd this response:
My eyes, once bright as a fire of thorns in hell,
are wizened as waterskins at a scum-choked well.
But blurred as they are, my eyes can pounce
and calibrate my supper to the final ounce,
and I dine on both believer and on infidel!

Jaham cocked his rifle. He felt strength return,
as though lament were fuel for old age to burn.
But the wolf inched closer in that fiery solitude
and began to keen:
I who whelped my thousands am now time's eunuch,
castrato of vicissitude,
a mothball-pasha in a tattered tunic,
howling in his hebetude,
and forced to share the fire with a versifying mechanic,
I who once commanded the stony wastes of Thamûd!

The wolf stood up from his hollow by the fire.
He threw back his whitened snout.
A cracked complaint teetered from his throat
while his ribs swelled like a wheezing concertina
and his final molars clittered like a string of beads.
As he threaded the desert air with a yipping sorrow,
that night by the coals where they bickered to soothe one another,
in his howl, so quavering and prosodic, Jaham could hear
the history of a life given to the anonymous wind
and the history of his own days,
gnawed to a bone of song.

Adham Atones

"Wash me of my sins with ice water and hail!"
Adham beseeched, "Scrub me with frost and thorn!"
The sand could not scour Adham of his sins
and in the holy month of Rajab he rose up.
"I'll lick the iron," he informed Allah.
These fits came on him every year or so.
He packed his saddle bags with figs and cheese.
He ambled eastward heading for Liwa'
and as he rode, he haggled with Allah:
"Don't cool the sun for me, that ghoul!
See how she spreads her furnace-lips! Ha!
Send 'Izzat, send me Lât, send all your fiends
to winkle the rot from my soul's cavities…!"
He thirsted for abasement as he raged.
He wanted to surmount the prayer that's just
pleasurable calisthenics for the tongue.
He wanted to hold the mortifying knife
close to his ribcage. He wanted to puff alive
that ash-encumbered ember that we call the heart.

Translucency

Adham's true ambition was translucency
and when his ribs began to shine
like candle flame through a fingernail,
he felt an almost alabaster warmth
climb his esophagus.
                                        He put on wool
in August. The taut curls of his cloak
sweated. His collar bleated its reek.
He abstained from all bandannas and
from ice cubes. At night his heartbeat
goose-stepped in his chest. He couldn't
sleep but watched a comet scroll
the dusty peristyle of heaven overhead.

Inside, at last, from hunger and from stress,
he recognized his enemy, the sly
child. He even came to see
the innocence of evil, how it
doggedly insists on wanting what it wants.

Because of this, he lashed his brain with thorns
yet loved the thistle imprints of the lash.
Because of this, he put his temper through
punishing dressages till opacity
slowly began to shine, a horse in foam.

Punkish matter, once all gravity,
flickered with auroral
promise just as he
sizzled in the beeswax of translucency.

The Sweat of Adham

Jaham wondered at the chilly sweat
that collected on the forehead of his friend.
He kissed the sweat off with his lips
as it sprouted in fat drops on Adham's skin
and trickled to the corners of his eyes
and ran along the cheekbones to his chin.
The sweat of death was on his oldest friend.
The more the sweat steamed from his pores
the stiller Adham lay. He was a well
evaporating in the suck of noon.
He was a waterhole where vagabonds
scrounge the final droplets with their fevered mouths.
He was a wadi where the spring cascades
parch as they race among the grains of clay.
He lay there on his sodden bed
and all the veins along his bald head
writhed and swelled, they grappled
with his blood that still rebelled.

Jaham plucked the sprigs of sweat away.
He dabbed at the panic in Bald Adham's eyes
with cool caresses and with gnomic lullabies
and he chanted in his soft, falsetto voice
a solace of surahs from the August Book.
Adham gazed at him, then faintly said:
"I can't find Allah by my jugular..."

When Adham died, freshets of water ran
out of his eyelids and his bristly ears,
out of his caverned nostrils and his lips.
His shoulder-blades were sopping with his death.
And from his bright skull to his drenching toes
Adham turned into a salt flat where the sun
hacks its mirages out of dead men's bones.

Adham in the Torments of the Tomb

There was a coziness in being dead
Adham had not expected. Nestled in a shroud,
his head towards Mecca and his restless hands
girdled at his waist, with several
cubic feet of sand heaped over him,
he felt himself a kernel in a ripening date.
He heard his last friends overhead
gossip and sob beside his modest grave.
He heard Black Mary whoop and ululate.
He strained to catch the panegyric words
they lavished on his dwindling memory,
and if his blood still ran he would have blushed.
He gloated in the praises that seeped down
into the snuggled darkness of his tomb.
But as their voices faded, as their steps
receded from his final resting place,
Adham felt a stab of grief and then
the grave began to tighten, his tomb
began to squeeze, he felt himself a coin
pinched in the bony talons of a miser.
He tried to shout, his mouth was bridled shut.
He tried to move, his feet were fettered fast.
He tried to weep, his eyelids were weighed down
by double pebbles in death's discipline.
The sand was famished and he felt it suck
styptic and invincible and alkaline
till all that was a river in him died.

Two sudden angels now began to worm
into his confines. *Call me Munkar*,
said the first. He looked like a religious cop,
all barbed-wire beard and dim salacious eye.
My name's Nakir, the second said; he had a bland

turban speckled with food stains on his skull
like a lazy mufti chewing a bent toothpick.
Each had a ball-point pen
clipped to one pocket of his nylon robe
but their wings were down at heel
and needed servicing.

Welcome to Barzakh! chirruped plump Nakir
but Munkar piped up with, *What do you believe?*
Adham for the first time in his death
thought, *I believe it's hellish here.*
I believe in the sun and in the moon and stars,
I believe in the beauty of well-serviced racing cars…
But he responded, *I do testify*
there is no God but God
and Muhammad is God's messenger!

Not bad, said Nakir but Munkar pressed on:
Tell us, he wheedled, *about God's attributes.*
Are they substratal with His essential Self
or superadded to His Essence, hmmm?
Adham pondered that and then replied,
I think that I'll be many moons down here!
Munkar began to jab and Nakir knelt
on Adham's belly and he pummeled him.
Both angels worked him over most methodically
with kidney pokes and left hooks to the ribs
until he howled,
His attributes are additives to God's own fuel!

See what a little jostling can do? said Munkar
smugly. They gave Adham D+
but he had passed at last. He'd passed and yet,
it would be many moons before he went
over the razor's edge and the rim of flame.
It would be nestled eons till he stepped

out of the tightness of his resting place.
It would be epochs of impatience
tucked like an ancient seed inside the husk
of his sand-scooped tomb till Adham walked
out of the earth again, with all the dead,
to glimpse the farthest lotus tree and sip
from the cooling rivulets of Salsabîl.

Jaham Curses

After Bald Adham perished Jaham howled
at heaven for seven days and seven nights.
He damned the arrogance of destiny but
Mrs. Jaham said, *Think of Ayyûb!*
Think of his long-suffering and welcome fate!

Jaham rose up from his place of grief and spoke:
I damn fate with my words,
I damn him with my fingers and my toes,
I damn him with my eyelids and my chin,
and I damn him with my dick and testicles!
I say, *You scurvy and marauding cur,*
you rank fox who scarfs our darlings down,
I hate the way you grind up all our bones
and punch out all our teeth with slingshot stones.
I hate how you vandalize our last good looks
and even rifle our sorry savings books.
You spit out all our bones the way an owl
disgorges the fur and bones of little mice
after he's sucked a bellyfull of blood!

Mrs. Jaham got nervous. *Hush,* she said,
Hush! She knew how slyly destiny
will sniff at the keyholes and the window joists,
how avidly blind fate will press its ear
to the thin walls and strain to catch a curse,
how it eavesdrops on the sentences of men
and scavenges among their careless words,
how it hunches to listen, just below the lip,
and hides in the pleats of gowns to pounce upon
the mutinous flinches of our stubborn souls.
Her soft cool paw she set on Jaham's mouth,

her breasts that smelled of earth in early spring
she bared for his solace. He could taste
wild onion, colocynth, and chicory
in the mother-covenant of her spurting milk.

Allah Answers Jaham in the Days of Dust

Have you ever
studied the annelations in the grub worm's weird
caparison? Have you ever listed
the bristles in the cacomistle's beard
or numbered his whiskers?
Do you know where the bandicoot
whelps her bandicootlets? Can you recruit
the fennec, the jerboa, or the giant clam?
I am that I am I am:
that is enough for you
(you don't even know the secrets of the kinkajou!).

Consider the camel, *My*
design entirely. Consider how
her nubile nostrils can
asperge the sand: I came up
with that. Her popular hump
that wobbles as she strides
is *Mine* as well; the affluence
of fat she larders in that hump
speaks with oily eloquence of *My*
sovereign kindness for the sons of men.
Consider her virginal and lustrous eye
balls pavilioned with delicate fly-whisks
of lash, and the pools of her enigma
in amber irises that narrow as she ruminates
her cud. I am justly proud of this
invention of the camel. Consider her!
Consider her monarchical tuft
of tail, her ingot hoofs that ring
across the badlands and can spark a flint!

Consider how My camel-creature
rolls her lips back from her yellow teeth
and roars in her jubilance
whenever she sniffs a carrot or a watercourse!

Jaham, consider! It was I who shaped you
like a loving owlet on a sundown tree
who whistles hosannas to the stars of night.
I fashioned you like a jackal dog whose yips
buff the roughest stones and make them glad.
And I will hold you always in the covert of My eye.

Jaham Says Adham's Beads

This was his rosary of olive wood
whose ninety-nine black beads hang from a cord.
He bought it on the pilgrimage, while still a child,
and it always looped down from his grimy hand.

The rosary's repose is serpentine.
It lies in its fat black coils in asp encirclings
and viper-rippling rings
and when I pick it up the dark discs click

between my fingers as I breathe the names
God gave Himself before the world began:
Creator, Fashioner, Immortal One,
Enduring, Living, Mighty, Merciful...

The strand yields to my impatient hand
with staccato softness of its vocatives:
Victorious, Compassionate, O Listener!
Resurrecting and Extinguishing, Unique!

But I pray better with the voiced
beads of the rosary, and not with names.
My supplication's in my fingertip
that slides the awed wood down the hidden thread.

The Junkyard Vision of Jaham

In paradise the smell of engine oil
will undercut the roses. The carburetors
of Eden will distract the seraphim,
those jukebox lutanists in phosphate trees.
The vaporous hush of essences
at the pinging pump will cauterize
the contusions of love, and the houris all
will bask on velveteen and naugahyde
bucket seats in a Russian Leather breeze.

The camshafts of heaven will outlive the axle trees.
The music of the manifolds will gown the clouds.
I see the black-seamed fingertips of the mechanics
on the copper-coloured keys of their accordions
and hear the ditties of the pit-stops pool.
The music of paradise will be shirt-sleeved and cool
and brandish red bandannas of rough flannel.
The integrity of metals will marmorealize
fleeting affections yet be various.
Amber oils will coronate chrone impulses
and be steadfast at last.
                              The dark order
of the mechanisms of heaven will be intricate
and unending, bedewed with rich grease
and yet, withal, imbued by the love
of couplings and black
gaskets, the grit of the known
lingeringly delivered back to innocence.

Jaham Plans for the Disposal of his Remains

After the sun has sucked my last breath out
and stripped away the spittle from my lips
and blotted out the blackness of my eyes,
after the bony sun has bled me dry
and parched my skin of shoulder and of thigh,

after the wind has teazled out my hair
and whisked all music from my gritted chin
and pinched my loincloth and my BVDs
and dusted off the last speck of my sighs,

after the sands have filed my bones down fine
and buffered fingernails and toenails smooth
and scrimshawed all the ivory in my teeth,

after the rain has rinsed my sockets out
and racked my ribcage like a snooker set
and rivered all my sweat and semen down
into the fatherless and fainting sand,

offer my remnants to these modest friends:
the scarab and the jackal dog.

Let the vocal dog with scavenger address
disarticulate my skeleton
and gnosh and knacker all my little bones
in midnight yapperies of his furred confrères.
Then let the scarab roll their frugal turds
into one dark and compact ball of dung,
let the beetle roll me in a fuming sphere
across the dunes into a bramble's hug
and give back to the molecules I was
what thankfulness a thorn owes to the sun.

Jaham's Last Words

The imam was preaching when he read the verse:
Everything is perishing except His face.

The verse had always startled Jaham secretly.

The flies are perishing in bowls of milk.
The mice are dying in their labyrinths.
The heels of pilgrims with that darkly rosy
rim of skin that glimmers when they bow
are perishing, as are their vivid hands,
their kisses, and their singing salutations,
the puffs of ochre dust their sandals plume.
Even the sun is dropping in its den.

As he was perishing himself
the cloudy poet said
the two lines that made his epitaph:

I love everything that perishes,
everything that perishes entrances me.

A Note on Names:
The second syllable of Jaham is to be pronounced as a long 'a.' Adham is pronounced "Ad-ham", with stress on the first syllable.

JAHAM'S POETIC MANIFESTO
The Arabic word *khinzîr* means "pig," an animal unclean before the law.

JAHAM IN THE AUTUMN RAINS
The *baharjîyah* is the pot in which coffee is steeped among the Bedouin. *Jaham* means "clouds." The herdsman uses the call *hâb hâb* to drive his flocks.

BALD ADHAM
Dajjâl is an apocalyptic figure similar to the Anti-Christ.

JAHAM SERENADES A SNAKE
The *ka'ba* ("cube") is the cubical structure situated near the center of the great mosque of Mecca in which the sacred Black Stone is set and around which Muslim pilgrims circumambulate during the Pilgrimage.

BALD ADHAM & BLACK MARY
The *'abâya* is the black, full-length garment worn by women in Saudi Arabia.

JAHAM DECIPHERS THE SCRIPTS OF INSOMNIA
The names of short vowels in Arabic are *fatha* (a), *damma* (u), and *kasra* (i).

BALD ADHAM FALLS INTO HERESY
It seems clear that Adham has fallen into the old and pernicious

heresy of *tajsîm* ("corporealism") in which God's physical attributes are taken too literally.

ADHAM OVERHAULS AN OLD CAPRICE
The *hubârâ* is that noble game bird, the bustard.

THE JINN
The *jinn* are fiery, intelligent beings whom God created from "a smokeless flame," according to Qur'an 55:15. *Bunn* is Arabic for coffee bean or coffee. The *sukûn* is the orthographic sign for a vowelless consonant.

RAMADAN
Here Jaham reveals himself to be a follower of the early Sufi master Abu al-Husayn al-Nuri.

JAHAM PRAISES
Jaham's lauds betray the influence of the Mu'tazilite school of theology which taught that even the most contemptible aspects of creation reveal God's goodness and mercy.

JAHAM ON THE DIFFICULT BEAUTY OF THE FIRST WHITE HAIR
Al-Sharif al-Radi was a great Shi'ite poet who died in Baghdad in 1016. The last line is my variation on one of his verses.

CALIPH OF CONFUSION
Iblîs (a corruption of Greek *diabolos*) is the devil.

ADHAM ATONES
'Izzat and Lât were pre-Islamic divinities.

ADHAM IN THE TORMENTS OF THE TOMB
Munkar and Nakir are the two angels who interrogate the dead in their tombs, according to traditional Muslim eschatology. *Barzakh* is the purgatorial limbo where the dead await the Last Judgment. *Salsabîl* is one of the fountains of Paradise.

Jaham Curses
Ayyûb is Job, honoured as a prophet in Islam.

Jaham's Last Words
The verse the imam reads is Qur'ân 28:88.

ACKNOWLEDGEMNTS

Many of these poems first appeared, often in different versions, in the following journals, to whose editors I am grateful: *The Boston Review, Descant, The Fiddlehead, The Malahat Review, The Paris Review, Parnassus, The Southwest Review* and *The Yale Review.*

For several details of desert life I am indebted to Alois Musil's classic work *The Manners and Customs of the Rwala Bedouins* (New York: American Geographical Society, 1928).

I am grateful to several friends who read drafts of the manuscript of *Araby* and gave me the benefit of their acumen, in particular, Ben Downing, Marius Kociejowski, Norm Sibum, and David Solway. I wish especially to thank Carmine Starnino, my editor, for his constant encouragement and sage advice.

My wife Irena, as always, helped me to strengthen and sharpen the collection markedly and I have benefited from her insight and sense of style.

Signal
EDITIONS

Edited by Carmine Starnino
Founding editor: Michael Harris

THE SIGNAL ANTHOLOGY Edited by Michael Harris
MURMUR OF THE STARS: SELECTED SHORTER POEMS Peter Dale Scott
WHAT DANTE DID WITH LOSS Jan Conn
MORNING WATCH John Reibetanz
JOY IS NOT MY PROFESSION Muhammad al-Maghut (Trans. by John Asfour
    and Alison Burch)
WRESTLING WITH ANGELS: SELECTED POEMS Doug Beardsley
HIDE & SEEK Susan Glickman
MAPPING THE CHAOS Rhea Tregebov
FIRE NEVER SLEEPS Carla Hartsfield
THE RHINO GATE POEMS George Ellenbogen
SHADOW CABINET Richard Sanger
MAP OF DREAMS Ricardo Sternberg
THE NEW WORLD Carmine Starnino
THE LONG COLD GREEN EVENINGS OF SPRING Elisabeth Harvor
FAULT LINE Laura Lush
WHITE STONE: THE ALICE POEMS Stephanie Bolster
KEEP IT ALL Yves Boisvert (Translated by Judith Cowan)
THE GREEN ALEMBIC Louise Fabiani
THE ISLAND IN WINTER Terence Young
A TINKERS' PICNIC Peter Richardson
SARACEN ISLAND: THE POEMS OF ANDREAS KARAVIS David Solway
BEAUTIES ON MAD RIVER: SELECTED AND NEW POEMS Jan Conn
WIND AND ROOT Brent MacLaine
HISTORIES Andrew Steinmetz
ARABY Eric Ormsby

 Véhicule Press

www.vehiculepress.com

CPSIA information can be obtained
at www.ICGtesting.com
Printed in the USA
JSHW021442200722
28295JS00001BA/8